Muldoon's "Library" of Limericks

Volume 1

by Seamus Muldoon

Copyright 2017 by Muldoon Publishing

All rights reserved under U.S. and international copyright law. Published by Muldoon Publishing via CreateSpace.com an Amazon company

ISBN-13: 978-1981167814
ISBN-10: 1981167811
CreateSpace title number: 7843127

Muldoon's Library of Limericks, Vol. 1, ed. 1

This edition published by arrangement with CreateSpace, 2017

INTRODUCTION

They say that puns are the lowest form of humor and limericks are the lowest form of poetry. You can add in the fact that political satire is the lowest form of social discourse. When you combine all three you get a literary form that can only come from the Library of Seamus Muldoon. This anthology of limericks was mostly written over the timeframe of 2016 and 2017, although some of the topics are timeless. The wide-ranging topics include modern day politics, ribald potty humor, art critique in limerick form and topics ripped from today's headlines.

This is not a book intended to be read in one sitting. In fact I highly recommend taking it in limited doses, to allow the individual rhymes and "punch lines" to have full effect. Too many limericks at a time can dull your mind, as evidenced by the current state of my own formerly sharp intellect. Therefore, this book should make a perfect "bathroom book". This is a book you should read in five to ten minute increments. Unless your particular bathroom needs are lengthier, three or four limericks at a time should suit you just fine.

What is a limerick? A limerick is a well-known and generally widely recognized form of short verse, usually thought of as doggerel. Typical limericks has a form of five lines, with the first, second and fifth lines longer and consisting of 8-10 syllables and sharing an ending rhyme, while the third and fourth lines have fewer syllables and share a different ending rhyme.

Limericks are generally thought of as humorous, with clever wordplay, ribald humor or both. They sometimes enter into the realm of the obscene, although I try to steer clear of the more blatantly coarse forms. That being said, I am not a prude, and hope that you aren't either.

I don't claim that all the word play in my limericks is original. In fact, I often take the punch line of a familiar joke and incorporate it into a limerick. Some of the puns in this book are far from original. I do seek to construct a novel and unique usage of even the oldest of puns, and any similarity to other limericks is not intentional. Some of the limericks are accompanied by a short blurb of background information to help set the stage.

I am not a poet. I am not a purist. Some of my limericks do not follow traditional form. Some of the jokes are best appreciated by ear rather than eye. I encourage readers to not only move their lips when they read, as I know most limerick fanciers do, but to actually read out loud, in order to pick up the meter. This will also help you appreciate the wordplay, some of which may be quite subtle and nuanced (or, as some have described it "heavy-handed and common"). Reading out loud will also discourage passersby from approaching too closely as they are likely to think you are insane. Hopefully however, you will not be bothered by people casually walking by as you read in the bathroom.

These are not your grandfather's limericks about Nantucket and ladies riding tigers. Look for hidden layers upon layers. Even the titles are sometimes jokes in and of themselves. At the end of the day however, do not seek wisdom here, instead, seek a little fun. I cannot protect you from the consequences of laughing out loud or audibly groaning. That burden falls squarely on your shoulders. Finally, even my typographical errors are intentional and add to the multi-layered humor.

If you are a person who is easily offended, or if you have an inflexible political ideology you may not be the right sort of person to be reading a book of limericks. As pointed out above, limericks are the lowest form of poetry. If you find yourself becoming offended, you should promptly terminate your immediate endeavors and return when you are in a receptive frame of mind. Make sure to flush and wash your hands.

So, without further ado I present to you, in no particular order, the first volume of Muldoon's Library of Limericks. I hope you enjoy reading them as much as I have enjoyed crafting them.

Seamus Muldoon
Colorado
December 2017

WHAT THIS COUNTRY
NEEDS IS
COMMON SENSE
PUN CONTROL

-1-

****

DISORIENTED

In China you'll see quite a sight
Manmade isles on the left and the right
If they tried this in Britain
It just wouldn't be fittin'
As they say, two Wongs can't make a Wight.

****

-2-

****

UNDEREXPOSURE

At a haunted house I had a peek

A photo of a ghost I did seek

The picture wasn't thrilling

Though the spirit it was willing

Sad to say, it seems the flash was weak

****

-3-

****

THE HARD-OF-HEARING APPRENTICE

My assistant's no good in the clinch
He can screw up a sure lead pipe cinch
"Hey Larry, you fool
You got the wrong tool!
That's a Vise-Grip™, I asked for a wench!"

****

-4-

****

'NETHER' LANDS INDEED

A certain young Amsterdam drinker
Turned out to be really a stinker
He slipped her a julep
And grabbed at her tulips
Forever was known as 'Hands Brinker'

****

-5-

****

NOW PLAYING – THE CARPENTERS

A carpentry showman named Jack
Took his show on the road, it's a fact!
He strips to bare wood
Sands and stains it real good
Then closes with his varnishing act!

****

-6-

****

GRAVITY WINS

The orthopedic surgeon was willin'
But my painful flat feet are still killin'
The pain is complete
Agony of defeat
I'm brought down by an evil arch villain

****

-7-

****

PESTILENCE RIDES A PALE HORSE

An old country vet named Doc Phipps
Found a cure for a rare equine grippe
He heals sores of the mouth
Now he's known through the South
The pox-man of the poor horse's lips

****

-8-

****

FIRST BASE AT LAST

He struck out when dating Cecilia
Had no better luck with Amelia
He joined the police force
And had better luck of course
He was finally copping Ophelia.

****

-9-

****

HALL AND OATES

The duo was not known to gloat
But once on a luxury boat
When John split his britches
Darryl had him in stitches
Seems Hall was just sewing his Oates

****

-10-

****

YOU ARE WHAT YOU EAT

There once was a man from Laredo
With a body shaped like a potato
After dinner he moaned
To the chef he intoned:
"I ate too much pasta, Alfredo!"

****

-11-

****

HELPING CHILDREN GO STRAIGHT

It seems there is a certain inefficiency
That led this crooked lad into delinquency
Ah, I've got the ticket!
The kid has the rickets
(He suffers from a vitamin D-ficiency!)

****

-12-

****

SCRIPTURE

Here's the sweetest trick-or-treating truth

The rules for giving candy to youth

I think that you are liable

To find it in the Bible

Chapter Seven - Book of Baby Ruth

****

-13-

****

MISSION SECURITY

At a zinc mine down by the strip
The foreman was Louis Von Phipps
He gives written approval
Before ore removal
The moral: Lou's slips? Zinc ships!

****

-14-

****

THE SCALES OF JUSTICE

From the time that Gil Finn was a boy
He thought bein' a fish would bring joy
He once made a wish
To be a goldfish
It turns out he was just being koi

****

-15-

****

FORGED IN FIRE

She had a cool sharpness to her touch
With a keen piercing gaze, like and such
She gave her blade a flick
And cut me to the quick
And calmly said, "Shank you very much!"

****

-16-

****

SHUTTING DOWN THE CIRCUS

The clowns heard the news and got drunk

The tumblers flipped out, who'd a-thunk?

The tears fell like rain

Now they're loading the train

As the elephants pack up their trunks

****

-17-

****

GO FOR THE JUGGLER

Closing the circus, making your escape
Taking down all of the bunting and crepe
To lay off all the troupe
You must jump through lots of hoops
Lest the contortionists get bent out of shape

****

-18-

****

IF AT WHIST YOU DON'T SUCCEED

A card playing man known as Blackjack McNess
Whose life was an absolute horrible mess
Failed at poker, gin and rummy
Failed at bridge, (he was no dummy)
But now he's reached the pinochle of success

****

-19-

****

FOODIES

If you've ever read an Asian restaurant blog
It's as easy as a-fallin' off a log
If you want to get down to it
We can teach you how to do it
C'mon let me show you how to wok the dog!

****

-20-

****

FILLER

The butcher at the end of the street

With supermarkets just can't compete

To keep his budget leaner

He put sawdust in his wieners

'Cause it's too hard to make both ends meat!

****

-21-

****

FLANDERS FEELZ

A Dutch hooker with nary a blemish
Had a Frenchman who stayed 'til the finish
She was heard to emote
"I've a Frog in my throat,
So excuse me, I'm just a bit Phlegmish".

****

-22-

****

RAPE AT THE GAS STATION

A dude in the town of South Bethel
Caught up in a major kerfeffle
At the local gas station
A vile allegation
The indictment read, "Who pumped Ethyl?"

****

-23-

****

WE'LL HAVE NUN OF THAT!

The madam was yelling "Dagnabbit"
If you must cop a feel then just grab it.
But don't ask the nun
If she wants to have fun
She won't let you get in the habit.

****

-24-

****

SPLISH SPLASH!

There once was a man named McNoodle

In a rainstorm, (a real dipsy-doodle!)

It rained dogs and cats

So he put on his hat

Went outside and stepped in a poodle!!

****

-25-

****

YELLOW BRICK ROAD - GEICO EDITION

The Woodsman has axes and saws
The Lion has naught but his paws
Still Dorothy can't dispute
A chameleon so cute.
That wonderful lizard of "Awwws!"

****

-26-

****

OLD GLORY

A street urchin captain named Raef
Knew th' streets of th' city weren't safe
On the flagstone, (what luck)
Met a match girl with pluck
"God protect her, and long may she waif!"

****

-27-

****

CAMPAIGN SLOGAN

A hunter named Tyler Magoo
Shot a moose while in his canoe
But the shot was cross-wise
Thus he met his demise
Tipped the canoe, and Tyler too.

****

-28-

****

SNEAKY LITTLE BASTIDGE

That flower salesman known as McGee
Camouflaged himself down to his knees
Then he went out in the woods
Where he tried to sell his goods
But we can't see the florist for the trees

****

-29-

****

NOR WAY, DUDE!!

I think that I now can report it
In Oslo cuisine is quite Nordic
But it sure isn't cheap
Along the coasts it's so steep
That most people just can't a-fjord it!

****

-30-

****

OH GIVE ME A HOME

Once all of the bison were killed
The sounds of the Great Plains were stilled
Now who'll pay the cost
For the lives that were lost?
We'll send them the buffalo bill.

****

-31-

****

BUT THEY DID GET A NICE FRUIT BASKET

The deer fell in love with an antelope
They were wed by Reverend Stanleyhope
All their friends got the blues
When they heard the big gnus
"Why do it in church?" "Well, we cantaloupe!"

****

-32-

****

IT'S NOT YOU, IT'S ME

The poor young lass is moping. She's a fretter.
Whatever could have possibly upset her?
I think perhaps one factor
Is they've repossessed her tractor
And felt compelled to send a John Deere letter!

****

-33-

****

HOT LUTE LICKS

The lute player's not one to boast

He's really much better than most

While she slices her bread

He says, "Dear Winifred?

"Do you want some jam with your toast?"

****

-34-

****

PYRAMID SCHEME

Studying ancient Egypt I would wager

Is a field of study posing some danger

While learning ancient plumbing

You surely risk becoming

An independent Pharaoh faucet major

****

-35-

****

SADDLE UP

The horse soldier tried to explain
A catchphrase will help you sustain
The best ones, of course
Come from your horse
"Giddy Up!" and "Remember the Mane!"

****

-36-

****

WEDDING VOWS

I say this from deep in my heart

I've loved you, yes, right from the start

But the mortgage you've carried

Means we'll have to stay married

At least until debt do us part

****

-37-

****

CANNERY ROW

A poor man who looked rather scruffy

His fish-cleaning job was a toughie.

But he gutted it out

As he said, with a pout

"I just need a diamond in the roughie!"

****

-38-

****

IT'S A TYPE OF HAT

An archeologist from Andorra
Sported nice hats, b'gosh and b'gorra
That dude Indiana Jones
Looked good while diggin' bones
He's known as Fedora the explorer

****

-39-

****

ADVICE FROM BILBO'S BIRTH MOTHER

Don't drink from a wine-filled goblet

If you lust in your heart, just stop it!

Don't lie, smoke or curse

Or recite doggerel verse

In short, adopt no bad hobbits!

****

-40-

****

AFFIRMATIVE ACTION IN THE SHIRE

I have this news on really good authority
Promotions not on merit or seniority
Frodo turned the job down
At the moment he found
That he was just a tolkien minority

****

-41-

****

PENICILLIN IN THE PERRIER?

I'd like to make one small correction

And point it in Meryl's direction

Hollywood is sick

But this "One Simple Trick"

Will clear up the worst streep infection.

****

-42-

****

WHERE'D YOU STASH THE LUTE?

He played as if his fingers were on fire
And hoped her fevered passion to inspire
She said "Wait a minute mister!
I saw you with my sister!
You're nothing but a dirty stinking lyre!"

****

-43-

****

CLICK YOUR HEELS THREE TIMES

Wherever Svetlana did roam

By air, on the land, sea or foam

She constantly pined

For the dwarf left behind

She knows that there's no face like gnome

****

-44-

****

TAKE A LOOK IN THE MIRROR, BUB

Narcissus showed great self-affection
He didn't deal well with rejection
But all the self-admiring
Soon became rather tiring
He quit, (upon further reflection)

****

-45-

****

ON OUR WAY TO NEW ZEALAND

This portrayal may not be correct
But it's the best that I can recollect
While transporting our flocks
The frigate hit the rocks
"Lord help us for we've been sheep-wrecked!!!"

****

-46-

****

DO WHAT YOU GOTTA DO

Said the lovely young maid in distress
This shipwreck's placed me under duress
But the fact is (did I mention?)
A better way to get attention
They'll save me sooner if I'm undressed!

****

-47-

****

NEAT!

Cap'n Morgan got the biggest of shocks
When his boat, inward bound, missed the docks
As the mizzen mast fell
He said, "Oh, what the hell!"
"I need a drink, but my rum's on the rocks!"

****

-48-

****

CAN THEY HEAR US NOW?

All the hopes of the shipwrecked are risin'
For a rescue ship's on the horizon
But that faraway schooner
Could've been hailed much sooner
If they'd got their cell phones from Verizon

****

-49-

****

LET'S OLD SPICE THINGS UP

At times I've a humor neurotic-al
And like to see art work erotic-al
Some girls of the Navy
Buxom, curvy and wavy
Would give us a view rather naughtical!

****

-50-

****

SOUNDS DIRTY BUT IT'S NOT

There once was a girl from Nantucket

Who carried her clams in a bucket

Eating oysters and mussels

Became such a tussle

Frustrated she muttered, "Just shuck it!"

****

-51-

****

FOR THE HALIBUT – FISHWIFE'S LAMENT

I can't stand the boredom much longer

The odor just keeps getting stronger

I smell like a fish

Oh dear how I wish

I never had wed the fishmonger!

****

-52-

****

CUBS WIN! CUBS WIN!

A hundred year drought? Gone mysteriously!
All Cubs fans are cheering deliriously
But now, after the hype
Fans don't have a gripe
They've finally taken the world seriously

****

-53-

****

GOTTA BREAK EGGS TO MAKE AN OMELET

There was a young man named Contreras

A cowboy from south of Los Cueros

While bull riding's nice

Please heed my advice

Look out for your huevos, rancheros!

****

-54-

****

INSECTICIDE IS NOT A SIN

At the parish potluck one fine day

There were bugs in the kale, so they say.

"Dear Lord", said the nuns

"What on earth can be done?"

Said the gardening priest, "Lettuce spray"

****

-55-

****

JUST A FLING

A chubby young man known as "Ponch"
An astronaut hardy and staunch
At his workplace one day
On his friend's trebuchet
Hung a sign that said, "Out to launch"

****

-56-

****

YOU"VE GOT YOUR FATHER'S NOSE

As a moose I know I look scary

My limbs they are so long and hairy.

The folks in my family

Say I'd look just like Bambi

If not for an active pituitary

****

-57-

****

THE INNKEEPER'S LAMENT

In England a dark storm was raining like piss
Gawain needed a ride, his horse was amiss
But the inn had no steeds
Just a St. Bernard breed
And who'd send a knight out on a dog like this?

****

-58-

****

ENNUI

My primary school years are gone!
Thoughts of music class still linger on
Instead of adoring
We kids found it boring.
We'd all play the zither and yawn

****

-59-

****

RARE BIRD

A bird fan from North Carolina
Had a cockatoo, he named it Dinah
His neighbors heard it talking
Wondered whose bird was squawking
"Well don't look at me, it's not mynah!"

****

-60-

****

GRILL

I was looking for something to eat
And discovered a barbecue treat
Now say what you will
When we fire up the grill
As they say, you just can't beat our meat

****

-61-

****

BREAKFAST

Though some folks might say I'm a nutter
Here's something to make your heart flutter
Baby goat as a spread
Would go well on your bread
Dry toast with just a little butter!

****

-62-

****

BAD PROGNOSIS

The Kraut ordered sausage at first
He ate 'til he thought he would burst
Then when he was full
He ate a seagull
And then took a tern for the wurst!

****

-63-

****

DON'T BLAME ME

Seismologists say, "Oy gevalt!"
The West Coast is under assault
If an earthquake should sway us
To quote San Andreas
"It certainly wasn't MY fault!"

****

-64-

****

HIKING ADVICE - PART ONE

When hiking it's really a snap

Avoiding the Lyme disease trap

This one simple trick

Will protect you from ticks

Encase yourself in bubble wrap!

****

-65-

****

HIKING ADVICE - PART TWO

So bubble wrap eases your cares

Prevents tick bites (Really, I swearz!)

And in spite of the fuss

An additional plus--

The popping sound chases off bears!

****

-66-

****

HIKING ADVICE - PART THREE

Now that you've got these ideas in your head

You still want a varmint free option instead

The super best way

For a pest free day?

Gosh, don't go hiking, just stay home in bed!

****

-67-

****

LET THEM EAT CAKE – PART ONE

Marie! That irrepressible kid!
I remember the things that she did
But the strangest I've seen
'Twas when she met Guillotin
Mademoiselle Antoinette flipped her lid!

****

-68-

****

LET THEM EAT CAKE – PART TWO

Marie Antoinette grew no older
Arrested by Citizen Soldiers
But whate'er you might say,
Up until her dying day
She had a good head on her shoulders

****

-69-

****

LET THEM EAT CAKE – PART THREE

Picture the Reign of Terror if you can
(Of Robespierre I've never been a fan)
But as Rudyard Kipling said
If you can keep your head
While others lose theirs, then you'll be a man

****

-70-

****

NONESUCH

An erstwhile street hooker named Hemphill
Found peace in a nunnery, 'twas simple
She forsook her former friends
And thus her sinful era ends
No, not with a bang, but a wimple

****

-71-

****

DENTISTRY – PART ONE

A dentist who lived in the south
In winter began to have doubts
If you haven't guessed
Why he felt so depressed
He always was down in the mouth

****

-72-

****

DENTISTRY – PART TWO

A charming young woman named Beth
Had horrible terrible breath
Her teeth all fell out
Now she's angry, no doubt
Watch out or she'll gum you to death!

****

-73-

****

DENTISTRY – PART THREE

An overambitious dental youth
Tried his best though he was quite uncouth
He inflicted such depravities
When he tried to fill in cavities
His boss said, "You can't handle the tooth!"

****

-74-

****

DENTISTRY – PART FOUR

An old dental expert named Booth
Regretted the loss of his youth
He shed many tears
'Cause he'd practiced for years
Alas he was long in the tooth

****

-75-

****

DEEP THOUGHTS

Imagine your udder surprise

Your milk bath guy oversupplies

As quick as you please

It'll be up to your knees

Then next thing you know, past your eyes.

****

-76-

****

HISTORIC EVENT AT THE HENHOUSE

Two chickens from south Adelaide
Were shocked and bewildered one day
When a large piece of fruit
Rolled down the chute
"Wow, just look at the orange momma laid!"

****

-77-

****

CRY FOWL, LET SLIP THE HENS OF WAR

My father had an interesting notion
'Bout a volatile hen feeding potion
Then sadly one night
All the fumes did ignite
Seems that's how you put poultry in motion

****

-78-

****

DELUSIONS

A poor country bumpkin named Meggs
He thought he had real chicken legs
His family neglected
To have this corrected
It turns out they needed the eggs.

****

-79-

****

MORE DELUSIONS

The claims of that chicken-man, Brewster
Just troubled his wife, it confused her
She pleaded, she begged
"If you're fowl, lay an egg!"
He said, "Don't be daft, I'm a rooster!"

****

-80-

****

IT'S A CINCH

To form an hourglass shape you must find
A strong corset of just the right kind
But you'll make a strange sight
If you cinch it too tight
A waist is a terrible thing to bind

****

-81-

****

ABSINTHE WITH A TWIST

At the Moulin Rouge, young mistress Wanda
Partied hard with her pal Peter Fonda
They made sounds when passing gas
Like a scooter up their ass
Absinthe sure doth make the fart go "Honda!"

****

-82-

****

LARGE SCALE PARENTING

An optimistic giant named Yarrow
Had a boy who was thin as an arrow
Stayed in his room, wouldn't eat
Broken bones or bloody meat
But hey, the son'll come out, for marrow!

****

-83-

****

BREAD

As any poor baker ought to know

Desperation can lay you down low

Temptation is a beast

West is west, yeast is yeast

I did it 'cause I kneaded the dough!

****

-84-

****

I LIKE MINE AL DENTE

A southern gal known as Joanie Pitts
Wants a man who's as good as it gets
For marital hominy
Her best husband nominee
Just has to be a man with true grits

****

-85-

****

FAITH (THREE CLERICS IN A BOAT)

The priest walked from the boat to take a dump
The pastor did the same without a bump
But when the rabbi tried he splashed
Sputtered up, somewhat abashed
They hadn't told him 'bout the cypress stumps

****

-86-

****

PUBLIC RESTROOMS AT NIAGARA FALLS

If you didn't raise the seat when you pissed

I must ask you to cease and desist

It's despicable at best

And it always leaves a mess

Signed, "Yours Truly, the Maid of the Missed"

****

-87-

****

UNIVERSITY WEATHER STUDIES

In college on chilly days like these
You have to be careful not to freeze
Whether you study climatology
Or major in meteorology
It's only a matter of degrees

****

-88-

****

DESSERTS

Our desserts, surely none can compare
They are just delicious, I declare
Peach cobbler, I've found
Tastes best when it's round
The converse of course? Pie are square!

****

-89-

****

INBREEDING

I say this without any malice
They got a genetic analysis
Seems the chromosome count
Was some oddball amount
That must mean it's Buckingham Palace

****

-90-

****

DISNEY PRESENTS "THE ORPHAN PRINCE"

Prince Charles? Well he's one of those
Whose ears weren't the ones that he chose
I think if he'd try
He could probably fly
If a feather were held in his nose

****

-91-

****

SHE SMILES FOR A REASON

What a charming (though clueless) young miss
But I have a few thoughts about this:
She stands there a while
With her radiant smile
Proving what they say "Ignorance is bliss!"

****

-92-

****

UNBEARABLE

A Canadian Network reporter
Tells a story 'bout north of the border
Two bears, so they say
Ate his girlfriend one day
Seems she suffered bi-polar disorder!

****

RIPPED FROM THE HEADLINES

HEADLINE: In 2017, James Jupp, a scholar of critical white studies, articulated his commitment to the destruction of "Whitestream cherished knowledge" in an article published for the "White Scholars Working Against Whiteness" issue of the journal Whiteness and Education.

-93-

****

RACISM IS ONLY SKIN DEEP

The scholarly white man, James Jupp

Said Whiteness is naught but corrupt

It's a laughable premise

As he admits with a grimace

"It's bullshit, I just made it up!"

****

HEADLINE: During the 2016 Democratic presidential primary campaign it came to light that DNC acting chairman Donna Brazile got tipped off about a potential CNN town hall question and forwarded this information to Hillary Clinton's campaign.

-94-

****

THROW HER A LIFESAVER™

It seemed like a really big deal
With the Dem nomination to steal
Here's what I'm thinking
Her campaign was sinking
So they tossed her a buoy from Brazile

****

HEADLINE: Car transporting Fidel Castro's ashes keeps breaking down, soldiers have to get out and push. Hooray Communism!

-95-

****

MAKING GOOD TIME

During Castro's final pass before the nation
They got hung up on his way to veneration
"We'll be there in a flash
'Cause we're really hauling ash
If you'll help us push it to a service station!"

****

HEADLINE: *In May 2017 President Donald Trump fired FBI director James Comey.*

-96-

****

ADD INSULT TO INJURY

Said Donald J. Trump to James Comey,
"I've got some bad news for you, Homey!
Since you've now been harpooned
Let's rub salt in the wound--
You're fired, but first. . . you will blow me!"

****

-97-

****

PARLIAMENTARY TERMINOLOGY 101

The Senate has finally been mustered
As usual it seems like a cluster
The Dems are demanding
Repubs are grandstanding
It ought to be called "full o' bluster"

****

-98-

****

I'VE GOT A BEEF WITH GAIA – PART ONE

Hey Folks! Have you all heard the latest?
Some guy took this chance to berate us
(Now stifle your mirth)
Seems we're killing the earth
With excessive bovine-style flatus

****

-99-

****

I'VE GOT A BEEF WITH GAIA – PART TWO

It's likely that he speaks from the heart
But he had it wrong right from the start
Amidst the cow splatter
The fact of the matter
Is the world thrives on Herefordshire farts!

****

HEADLINE: Drug-fueled sex orgy at Furry convention

-100-

****

OOOOO...KLAHOMA

They partied and they never planned to stop

It got so wild that someone called the cops

The scene was so exciting

That we thought we should go riding

On the furry with the syringe on top

****

HEADLINE: Ohio governor John Kasich made a run for the Republican Party presidential nomination in 2016. He attempted to tap in to mainstream America by touting his working-class roots.

-101-

****

NEITHER RAIN NOR SNOW

O'er yonder's a gathering gale, man
It threatens of lightning and hail, man
I can handle bad weather
My sack's made of leather
I am Kasich! The son of a mailman!!

****

HEADLINE: *"The Science Is Settled: Veganism Can Be Lethal for Children"*

-102-

****

TRUST YOUR INSTINCTS

He won't eat them all by himself

You can't sneak them in using stealth

This article just shows

What a five-year-old knows

Vegetables are bad for your health!!

****

HEADLINE: The year 2017 brought wave after wave of allegations of sexual misconduct in Hollywood, the media, Congress and the business world.

-103-

****

MORALLY BANKRUPT

A Hollywood producer named Mears
Admitted he'd been bugg'rin' for years
But those office 'romances'
Have ruined his finances
And he's now left his firm in arrears

****

HEADLINE: Cher to star in a movie about the Flint, Michigan water crisis.

-104-

****

EXHIBIT ONE, YOUR HONOR

The water in Flint is a waste
I think it should just be replaced
We should do something 'bout it
And if you might doubt it
Just look what it did to Cher's face!

****

HEADLINE: Jonathan Gruber, known as the architect of Obamacare, drew ire from political opponents with comments about being able to fool the average American voter easily because they just aren't very bright.

-105-

****

RUBES

He thinks that the "folks" are all goobers

With the mental prowess of tubers

But O-Care is just a farce

So that dude can kiss my arse

Sieg heil, Herr Gruppenfuhrer Gruber!

****

HEADLINE: Following his failed presidential bid in 2000, Senator Al Gore went into seclusion, only to emerge some time later as the new guru of the Man-Caused Climate Movement.

-106-

****

HE DOESN'T BELIEVE A WORD HE SAYS

Al Gore's a Gaia doctor (and I quoth)

The sickness and the cure, he's got 'em both

"The planet has a fevah!

Send me cash, I won't deceive ya

I swear it on my Hypocritic Oath!"

****

HEADLINE: In June 2016 billionaire activist Tom Steyer joined Al Gore on the global climate change scene, calling President Trump's withdrawal from the Paris Treaty a "traitorous act of war".

-107-

****

BILLIONAIRE ACTIVIST? NOW THAT'S RICH

Well this Paris thing's quite the development
Seems Al Gore is becoming irrelevant
Along with Thomas Steyer
They're both dirty stinkin' liars
Carbon footprints the size of an elephant

****

HEADLINE: *Environmentalist group advocates having actual physical sex with Mother Earth*

-108-

****

VOLCANIC ERUPTION

I went up in the mountains north of Duncan
I felt like I should do some boulder chunkin'
Now Gaia, being flirty
Told me "Do it, down and dirty!"
"Oh screw the Earth, I think I'll go spelunkin!"

****

HEADLINE: OPEC pleads with the U.S. to reduce its domestic oil production in order to help the world economy.

-109-

****

TO MARKET TO MARKET JIGGITY JIG

Ah, OPEC, that vile Gang of Twelve

Has oil reserves left on their shelves

If they still can't compete

Using their own crude sweet

Perhaps they should go frack themselves!

****

HEADLINE: Gun control advocates equate deer hunters in upstate Wisconsin to gang-bangers in urban areas.

-110-

****

A DEER BOY TURNING HIS LIFE AROUND

Lil' Bambi as a rapper was the best
The favorite in the 'hood from east to west
But one day a cheesehead hunter
Put our Bambi six feet under
Too bad he didn't wear his blaze orange vest!

****

HEADLINE: Genderqueer woman raises her seven year old son as a girl.

-111-

****

KING OF HEARTS

A poor confused lad known as Milam

Didn't know gender, species or philum

His queer-mother Pearl

Made him think he's a girl

The inmates now run the asylum

****

HEADLINE: Donald Trrump defeats Hillary Clinton in the 2016 Presidential election, upsetting the hopes of those seeking to elect the historic first woman President.

-112-

****

HILLARY'S CONCESSION SPEECH

Excuse me I've been out of touch

What with cursing and drinking and such

Let me say from the start

In the words of Max Smart

I missed it by just --><-- that much

****

HEADLINE: Donald Trrump defeats Hillary Clinton in the 2016 Presidential election, upsetting the hopes of those seeking to elect the historic first woman President.

-113-

****

COULDN'T QUITE BREAK THROUGH

The next morning we all had a feeling

About Hillary stumbling and reeling

But it's not like you thunk

She sure wasn't drunk

She'd just bounced off the Plexiglas ceiling!

****

HEADLINE: Donald Trrump defeats Hillary Clinton in the 2016 Presidential election, upsetting the hopes of those seeking to elect the historic first woman President. Some news outlets, anticipating a Clinton victory, jumped the gun with their reportage.

****

EXTRA! EXTRA!

At Newsweek the editors were fumin'

The wishfulness was simply unhuman

But they stuck to tradition

With their Hillary edition

A modern day "Dewey Defeats Truman"!

****

HEADLINE: Donald Trump defeats Hillary Clinton in the 2016 Presidential election, upsetting the hopes of those seeking to elect the historic first woman President. Many wondered how Mrs. Clinton would react to the great disappointment.

-115-

****

REMEMBER 2000?

Now here's a little tidbit I find weird

The rumors say that Hillary's disappeared

It's being said what's more

She's going to be like Gore

She'll gain a hundred pounds and grow a beard.

****

HEADLINE: Distraught mother of youth shot by an armed employee while robbing a Pizza Hut, exclaims that shooting an armed man during the commission of a felony should be the sole purview of the police.

-116-

****

DEEPER POCKETS

Darling Johnny robbed a pizza shop

Even though the boss told him to stop

Now she mourns her honey

She could've made more money

If only he'd been shot by a cop

****

HEADLINE: Transgender subjects being taught in elementary schools.

-117-

****

HORTON HEARS A XIM/XER

Are you puzzled by what you should be?

Are you he? Or a she? Or a xe?

Well if I get a choice

In my best grown-up voice

I'll declare, "What am I? I'm a me!!"

****

HEADLINE: Politician's unaccomplished neophyte offspring groomed to take up the political torch and carry it forward.

-118-

****

POLITICIAN'S DAUGHTER – PART ONE

She takes up the mantel with alacrity

And nary a smidgen of hypocrisy

I've ne'er before seen

Someone burst on the scene

With pure meteoric mediocrity

****

HEADLINE: Politician's unaccomplished neophyte offspring groomed to take up the political torch and carry it forward.

-119-

****

POLITICIAN'S DAUGHTER – PART TWO

A numbnutz with condescending attitude

Bestrewing her path with stale beatitudes

A hideous loathsome creature

With carnival sideshow features

She's a walking talking duck-billed platitude!

****

HEADLINE *"Just after midnight on Tuesday, May 30 Donald Trump tweeted:* **"Despite the constant negative press covfefe..."** *The internet lit up with reactions to the tweet.*

-120-

****

COVFEFE

The President's tweet did announce it

The media quickly denounced it

It's a cultural sensation

That's sweeping the nation

But I still don't know how to pronounce it!

****

HEADLINE: "Bill Nye: Science Guy": Host of '90s kids' TV show turns his crusade to climate-change deniers

---

-121-

****

OH SO CLOSE, BILL

He wears a lab coat and bow tie.

And asks daring questions, like "Why?"

He looks like a nerd

And he uses big words

He's Bill, darn nigh a science guy!

****

HEADLINE: In early 2017 an expectant nation awaited the impending good news that April the Giraffe had finally given birth. And we waited. And we waited. And we waited. And we waited...

-122-

****

THE GIRAFFE'S LAMENT – PART ONE

The expectant giraffe is elated

(As so many observers have stated)

If she goes in the bushes

Gives a couple big pushes

She at last will be de-calf-inated.

****

-123-

****

THE GIRAFFE'S LAMENT – PART TWO

There's one thing of which there's no doubt

That baby giraffe's in a pout

And he isn't just joshin'

He'll proceed with caution

Not eager to stick his neck out!

****

-124-

****

THE GIRAFFE'S LAMENT – PART THREE

So our baby giraffe's still inside?
What's the deal? Is it all 'cause of pride?
So, what's it all about?
Can't entice the fella out?
Just fit the momma with a Slip-N-Slide!

****

*HEADLINE: 1 In 4 Democrats See GOP as **Existential** Threat to "Way of Life". . .*

-125-

****

AN OVERUSED WORD

When everything's 'leventy!! you can bet

The folks'll break out in a panic sweat

Boogeymen, don't you see

There's one behind each tree

Even puppies are an existential threat!!

****

HEADLINE: "Chinese Kung Fu master uses genitals to pull bus down street"

-126-

****

NOVEL PENIS ENLARGEMENT TECHNIQUE

Using his tool as a school bus puller

Made that Kung Fu guy's life so much fuller

But a more useful trick

Would be getting his dick

To go fetch fresh coffee and a cruller!

****

HEADLINE: On the first anniversary of the 2016 presidential election, people were invited to join in a "Scream at the Sky" protest, symbolizing resistance to the duly elected President.

-127-

****

TO BOLDLY GO

All round the globe the protest did reach

The stated intent? Trump to impeach!

People, let's get to work!

(In the words of James Kirk)

Everyone set your phasers to "Screech!"

****

HEADLINE: "94-year-old woman graduates college"

-128-

****

MOCHALATTA GRANNY

I'd like to tell a story to ya, mistah
About a nonagenarian sistah
She's pleased as she can be
That she got her new degree
Now she works as Starbucks' oldest barista!

****

POEMS ABOUT POEMS, ART AND SCIENCE

POEMS
On originality-

"Immature poets imitate; mature poets steal" – T.S. Eliot

-129-

****

LONGFELLOW'S CONFESSION

By the shores of old Lake Gitchee-Gumee
I once copied a poem off of my roomie
It turned out pretty funny
And I made lots of money
I said, "Yeah sure I stole it. So sue me!"

****

ART
Bob Ross was a popular artist who gave painting classes on TV. He was noted for his upbeat commentary, referencing "Happy little clouds" and such.

-130-

****

BOB ROSS - HOMAGE

"Happy Clouds" is more than a gimmick

It's a technique I've learned to mimic

Ross painted trees and birds

I do the same with words

Voila, a happy little lim'rick

****

POEMS
John Greenleaf Whittier's poem "Barbara Frietchie" tells of a ninety-year old woman who defied Robert E. Lee's troops marching through Maryland by insisting on flying the U.S. flag. Tough old broad! It's nice, but Whittier didn't go quite far enough!

-131-

****

AND GET OFF MY LAWN!

Up rose old Barbara Frietchie then,

Bowed with her fourscore years and ten;

A nonagenarian

Quite the contrarian

From the days when women were men!!

****

POEMS
A little learning is a dangerous thing,
Drink deep, or taste not the Pierian spring;
Where shallow draughts intoxicate the brain,
And drinking largely sobers us again.
- Alexander Pope

-132-

****

POEMS AND RIDDLES

I like Pope's poetical styling

It's clever, and witty. Beguiling.

But riddle me this

If ign'rance is bliss

Then why in the hell aren't I smiling?

****

ART
"Ecce Homo" by Elias Garcia Montoya made the news when a well-meaning but likely deranged church worker performed an ill-fated restoration.

-133-

****

BEHOLD MAN

An over-fastidious Major Domo

In the manner of old Greco-Romo

When he first met a gay

Didn't know what to say

So he recoiled and said, "Eek, a homo!"

****

SCIENCE

An abstract from a scholarly journal of sorts:
Corporal Hauntings (Re)membering Father by David Purnell
Depart Crit Qual Res, Vol. 4 No. 4, Winter 2015; (pp. 65-82)
"In this writing, fictionalized conversations take place with the hauntings of my child self during fragments of past experiences that I consider contributors to a failed familial relationship. Through this account, I suggest ways to redirect the narrative momentum that pushes narrative inheritance into the future."

****

THE SCHOLARLY METHOD

A scholar of remarkable mettle

Had a hogshead of hogwash to peddle

A familial apparition

Published in the next edition

Please don't doubt him, the seance is settled!

****

ART

The Storm by Pierre-Auguste Cot
This painting depicts a young couple fleeing an oncoming storm, with the damsel clad in a flimsy gown that leaves nothing to the imagination. It is thought to be based on an 18th century novel "Paul et Virginie"

-135-

****

ART APPRECIATION

The background is ominously stippled

The fabric is suggestively rippled

But lo and behold

The air must be cold

For that damsel's distinctively nippled

****

ART
The painting Elégante à l'Opéra by René Gruau depicts a woman leaning forward in an opera box, surveying the auditorium below. She has an impossibly narrow nose.

-136-

****

'TIS THE SEASON TO BE WHEEZIN'

At the risk of appearing hostile

I don't see how breathing is poss'ble

The shape of her face

Seems a bit out of place

Those must be the world's smallest nostrils!

****

ART
"Brothel" by Joachim Beuckelaer depicts a humorous scene at a brothel with several couples gropulating, some naked breasts, an acrobat doing a handstand and other assorted tomfoolery.

-137-

****

THE BREAST OF BOTH WORLDS

This painting seems quite Katzenjammer-y

With all sorts of wacky flim-flammery

But to quote Bob Hope

Re: this recurrent trope

I'd like to say, "Thanks for the mammaries!"

****

ART

-138-

****

ART IS JUST SHOW BUSINESS AFTER ALL

Surrealism seems like such folly
Just head-scratching nonsense, by golly!
But that young Salvador
Is one guy I adore
I'd just like to say "Hello, Dali!"

****

SCIENCE Asimov's Three Laws of Robotics.
1. A robot may not injure a human being or, through inaction, allow a human to come to harm.
2. A robot must obey orders given it by human beings except where such orders would conflict with the First Law.
3. A robot must protect its own existence as long as such protection does not conflict with the First or Second Law.

-139-

****

'I ROWBOAT' BY ASIMOV

When we first teach our rowboats to think

They and humans must all be 'in sync'

We must keep them in check

Lest there be a shipwreck

And all mankind ends up 'in the drink'

****

ART

"Mornex (Haute-Savoie) - Au Fond, Le Mole" by Jean-Baptiste-Camille Corot depicts a French countryside with several young women beside a freshly tilled plot of land, perhaps newly seeded.

-140-

****

AH'M FOND OF MOLES - PART ONE

Ah, a bucolic scene of French lasses

All their meals come from dirt and dry grasses

Their earth-based diet

Is so good, you should try it

'Cause their pancakes taste just like mole asses

****

ART
*"Mornex (Haute-Savoie) - Au Fond, Le Mole"
by Jean-Baptiste-Camille Corot depicts a French
countryside with several young women beside a
freshly tilled plot of land, perhaps newly seeded.*

-141-

****

AH'M FOND OF MOLES - PART TWO

The fields had been planted with flowers

Awaiting their fine April showers

But then came the invasion

Of moles, (mostly Eurasian)

At 10 to the 23rd power!

****

ART
A View Of The Thames With Saint Paul's Cathedral From Blackfriars

Henry Pether depicts the Thames River from underneath a stone arch bridge which frames the top and sides of the view. Two people stand in the moonlight.

-142-

****

UNDER THE STONE ARCH BRIDGE

The romantic young couple was willin'

On a walk by the river. Just chillin'

They discovered their error

In a moment of terror.

And fell prey to the dreaded Arch villain.

****

ART
"The Fighting Temeraire tugged to her Last Berth to be broken up, 1838" by Joseph Mallord William Turner depicts one of the last great sailing warships being towed to its final resting place by a small yet powerful steamship. This allegorical painting captured the feeling of the end of one era and the arrival of another.

-143-

****

IT'S AN ALLEGORY!!!

See our great ship of state's resignation

As it comes from its last battle station

As society burned

The tide may have turned

Now we witness the Berth of a Nation

****

ART
Fight For The Waterhole by Frederic Remington depicts several cowboys hunkered down around a desert water hole, rifles at the ready

-144-

****

HOPE SPRINGS

In this most desolate of all places

Those Indians are tryin' to erase us

I don't think they oughter

'cause a corpse in the water

Would just ruin this desert oasis.

****

ART
Young Girl Reading by Jean-Honoré Fragonard depicts a young girl in a bright yellow dress, reading. Her little finger looks odd.

-145-

****

HOPEFUL GIRL WITH BENT FINGER

The young girl's repose. So mellow.

The tint of her clothes? So yellow!

She sits there all thinky

With her malformed little pinky

Awaiting her beau. Fine fellow!

****

ART
"Starry Night" is one of Vincent Van Gogh's most well-known paintings. It depicts a night sky. With stars.

-146-

****

FLEETING IS THE NIGHTTIME

The stars in the sky before dawn
As nighttime is moving along.
I give you fair warning
It soon will be morning
Van Goghing, Van Goghing, Van Gone

****

ART
Drunken Silenus supported by Satyrs by Anthony van Dyck depicts a fat naked drunk old man supported by a troupe of various and sundry mythical creatures.

-147-

****

DRUNKEN ENTOURAGE

We Satyrs supporting Silenus

Are propping him up in between us

The flautist is tooting

And the Cupids "Woot-wooting"

While Pan sneaks a peek at his penis

****

ART
Phryne Devant L'areopage by Jean-Léon Gérôme depicts the trial of Phryne, an ancient Greek courtesan. Phryne was on trial for profaning the Eleusinian Mysteries, and is said to have been disrobed by Hypereides, who was defending her, when it appeared the verdict would be unfavourable. The sight of her nude body apparently so moved the judges that they acquitted her.

-148-

****

PHRYNE'S DEFENSE – PART ONE

A Greek defense attorney known as Drury
Staged his best defense with sound and fury
In an act of sheer despair
He flung her clothing in the air
The trial ended with a well hung jury.

****

ART
Phryne was on trial for profaning the Eleusinian Mysteries, and is said to have been disrobed by Hypereides, who was defending her, when it appeared the verdict would be unfavorable.

-149-

****

PHRYNE'S DEFENSE – PART TWO

She bribed the jury, setting up this scene
The first real naked girl they'd ever seen
"We rest our case, your honor"
Said the naked prima donna
'Tis Phryne, the original Drachma Queen

****

ART
Phryne was on trial for profaning the Eleusinian Mysteries, and is said to have been disrobed by Hypereides, who was defending her, when it appeared the verdict would be unfavorable.

-150-

****

PHRYNE'S DEFENSE – PART THREE

Phryne's clothing has gone all askance

As the jury could tell at a glance

She said to the men

"How's that?" "Come again?"

"Can I offer you guys a lapse dance?"

****

ART
"Alex on Pig" a painting by Bryten Goss, depicts a woman dressed only in black bra, panties and thigh-high stockings, riding a pig bareback.

-151-

****

I AM WOMAN, HERE'S ME BOAR

A feminist named Alex McComb

Rode a pig everywhere she did roam

The speed was subsonic

But I find it ironic

'Twas the *bacon* that brought *Alex* home

****

ART
"Alex on Pig" a painting by Bryten Goss, depicts a woman dressed only in black bra, panties and thigh-high socks, riding a pig bareback.

-152-

****

HEAD 'EM UP, MOVE 'EM OUT

The art world's going through a schism

Betwixt romance and surrealism

She rides down the trail

(With a curly-cue tail)

A new genre -- Romanti-chisholm.

****

ART
If abstract art were a limerick it would go something like this:

-153-

****

ON ABSTRACT ART IN GENERAL

There was a young man from colormumble

Who didn't know quite how to rectanglesmear

He swervy perspectived

And vague shapified

Hang on the wall this => side up.

****

ART

Lady Dog Lizard by James Rosenquist is an abstract painting that includes eyeballs, floral imagery and parallel lines. I didn't see a Lady, a Dog or a Lizard, but I did think of a limerick.

-154-

****

WE'RE NOT ON CANVAS ANYMORE, TOTO

I really like this picture, because

The daring technique gives me pause

The Lady's old news

And the dog evokes "Oohs"

But it's a wonderful lizard of "awwws"

****

SCIENCE
HEADLINE: "Feminist Researcher Proposes Bold New Science Mixing Quantum Mechanics and Intersectional Feminism"

-155-

****

THE PHYSICS OF HIGH HEELS

The feminist theory of Quantum

Those students, it's destined to haunt 'em

Two grad students at the mall

Succinctly summarized for all

"Those shoes! They're just darling! I want 'em!"

****

ART

-156-

****

I KNOW ART WHEN I SEE HIM

Mr. Linkletter has a big heart
On his TV show, doing his part
The kids that he brings
Say the Darndest Things
I don't care what you say, now THAT'S Art

****

ART
Mary Magdalene by Giovanni Girolamo Savoldo depicts Mary Magdalene. The most striking part of the painting is a shimmering metallic silver-colored cloak, splendidly rendered. The fabric makes the painting.

-157-

****

NEVER REACHING THE END

Giovanni's heritage is Latin

He's constantly be-boppin' and scattin'

The cloth looks like silk

Of a moody, blue ilk

And he draped all his knights in white satin

****

ART
On interpreting abstract art

-158-

****

PAINTED WHILE ON SAFARI

All those abstracted reds, greens and blues

Imagination will give you some clues

There's a zebra! Giraffes?

A hyena that laughs!

But I'm not going to fall for fake gnus.

****

ART

"Samson and Delilah" by Peter Paul Rubens depicts a sapped Samson collapsed in the lap of a bare-breasted Delilah after being shorn of his hair and stripped of his strength.

-159-

****

BURMA SHAVE

Samson, oh my dear where have you been?

And why are all your muscles so thin?

You ought to remember

You're not just a member

But President of the Hair Club For Men.

****

ART
"Samson and Delilah"

-160-

****

DO YOU EVEN LIFT, BROHEIM?

Our Samson had more muscle than brains
And he had a luxurious mane
But Delilah she gave
Him a trim and a shave
Now he no longer tells of his GAINZZ!

****

ART
"Samson and Delilah"

-161-

****

MAN'S GREATEST WEAKNESS

Sweet Delilah she showed us her tits

Said Samson, "That's as good as it gets."

She went to great lengths

To sap all his strength

"Get a shave and a haircut, two bits!"

****

ART
"Samson and Delilah"

-162-

****

WAXING POETIC

Said Delilah with treason reptilian
"Hey Samson, you should thank me a million"
You should've been at the gym
When I gave you that trim
Just be thankful it weren't a Brazilian!

****

ART
"Samson and Delilah"

-163-

****

BRRRRRRPPPPPTTT!!!

Samson hollered out (he gave a shout)
"I'm knackered! Of that there is no doubt."
Then he laid down in her lap
Just to take a little nap.
"Motorboatin' wears a fellow out!"

****

ART
"Samson and Delilah"

-164-

****

FEE FITTY FIE FITTY FO FITTY FUM

Said Samson as he nuzzled the titties
I'm the strongest man in this whole city
To Delilah's sheer frustration
I have practiced masturbation
Now? I clean and jerk about tree-fitty

****

ART
"Samson and Delilah"

-165-

****

GRAND FINALE

Samson, are you a man or a mouse?

Now you're under arrest, ya big louse!

Is it really that simple

To destroy a temple?

He's a hit! He just brought down the house!

****

SCIENCE
Alexander Graham Bell invents the telephone and our lives are changed forever.

-166-

****

JUST AS I WAS SITTING DOWN TO EAT

The estimable Alex G. Bell
Thought his phone was real nifty, just swell
Now I can't get through supper
Without some caller-upper
I hope that he is roasting in hell!

****

ART
"Sunrise" by Claude Monet depicts an early morning river scene through the haze of an industrial district. Two shadowy boats make their way down the river.

-167-

****

PIXELATION

The lighting is all mottled and stringy

You can barely discern those two thingies

I think I make out

With some room for doubt

It's a picture of Claude Monet's dinghy!

****

ART
Toulouse-Lautrec

-168-

****

LAUTREC'S OUTFIT

Please don't think I'm being obtuse
I'm not sure this fits my caboose
At first it felt right
And next 'twas too tight
And now, darn it all, it's toulouse!"

****

GENERAL-PURPOSE EVERYDAY RUN-OF-THE-MILL GARDEN-VARIETY LIMERICKS

-169-

****

METAMORPHOSIS, BEDBUG STYLE

There once was a vantz mit a shwantz
Who sought a sex change. What a ponce!
Now with a mangled ween
He knows the difference 'tween
What he needs; versus what he wants!

****

-170-

****

VACCINATION

A clever young lad known as Ken
At the doctor's when he was ten
Did that age old clinic dance
"Look away, drop your pants!
Bend over, here it comes again!"

****

-171-

****

WEIGHING HEAVY ON MY MIND

The broken scales of kindly old Doc Palance
No longer made a proper tare allowance
He didn't know what to think
So he shared it with his shrink
She said, "You're fundamentally unbalanced!"

****

-172-

****

A MILLION TO ONE SHOT, DOC

A young lad from Kalamazoo
Had sounds coming from his wazoo
He's pootin' and tootin'
All quite high falutin'
He'd landed right on his kazoo!

****

-173-

****

WHO NEEDS POT AT THIS ALTITUDE?

When I'm hiking up close to the sky
I feel giddy, and strange, and here's why
As I stroll through the trees
With a gasp and a wheeze
Hypoxia! The Rocky Mountain High!

****

-174-

****

HE MAKES A LOT, THEY SAY

Here's an item that you might find funny
Back when Elton's prospects weren't so sunny
Well, Madman 'Cross the Water
Sold better than it oughter
You're darn tootin' Levon likes his money!

****

-175-

****

GRAMPA AND GRAMMAR

His grammar is never definitive
When he's tense he'll parse your diminutive
But a dangled participle
Will hardly cause a ripple
He'll uses it to split your infinitive

****

-176-

****

CAP'N KNUTE ROCKNE

A mermaid can make you feel chipper

Like the crew of a fast Yankee clipper

So jump on your schooner

Prepare to harpoon 'er

Go out and "Win One for the Flipper!

****

-177-

****

TO THE BEST OF MY NOWLEDGE

Why the heck is knife spelled with a "K"?
You wouldn't want it any other way
It sounds knice and clever
To knever say knever
I have knext to knothing knew to say!

****

-178-

****

LIVING HIGH ON THE HOG

The contrast 'tween have-nots and haves
Just check out those men's better halves
See, that fat banker's wife
Had the time of her life
She sure has some fine, sturdy calves!

****

-179-

****

HOW TO MEDICATE A CAT- PART ONE

When you're giving a cat his eye ointment
Be prepared for a great disappointment
Since your arms he will shred
You had best plan ahead
With a pre-scheduled doctor's appointment!

****

-180-

****

HOW TO MEDICATE A CAT- PART TWO

The eye's infected. Maybe it's bubonic!
'Twas diagnosed by techniques ultrasonic!
To put meds in the eyes
You could try to hypnotize
It's the best way to give the cat a tonic

****

-181-

****

BURY ME WITH MY CAR

'Twas time for me to go and meet my Maker
I had some problems with the undertaker
Now I'm not bragging, kids
But he couldn't close the lid
Because I had a giant 'Studebaker'!

****

-182-

****

HOW DOES YOUR GARDEN GROW?

I'm not hip to that gardening scene
I'm the worst that you ever have seen.
As a gardener I'm dumb
I am nothing but thumbs
And not even one of them is green!

****

-183-

****

DIGGIN' UP BONES

Poor Francis was known for his thuggery
For mugging and all sorts of buggery
But he got into trouble
At a grave with a shovel
Engaged in pernicious skull-duggery

****

-184-

****

MEN OF A CERTAIN AGE

With all of this talk about competence

A broad metaphor for men's confidence

But I've come to that age

Where now all the rage

Is the mere act of maintaining continence.

****

-185-

****

"CACTUS JACK" GARNER

What does the vice president get?

A Presidential Medal. That's it.

For participation

And personification

'Tain't worth a warm bucket of spit!

****

-186-

****

THE CITATION READS (IN PART)

"For eight years acting in fine fettle
Mom-jeansing, skeet-shootin', bike pedal
Umbrella-stymied by a portal
Why you're so dang near-immortal
We award you this Participation Medal"

****

-187-

****

DOES THIS HAT MAKE MY HEAD LOOK BIG?

An obstreperous cowpoke named Nat

Shot a feller for calling him fat.

Now we know that ain't right

But Nat wasn't too bright...

Half-pint brain in a ten-gallon hat!

****

-188-

****

HARK

An angelic visitor aspired
As a comic perhaps to get hired
To Joseph and Mary he quipped
I've just flown in from E-gypt
And let me tell you my wings are tired!

****

-189-

****

POLITICS AS USUAL

Old McNabb has a penchant to gloat
You wouldn't want to be in THAT boat
Those compromising pics
Will sure do the trick
If he ever has to blackmail a goat.

****

-190-

****

I NEVER DID LIKE THAT MOVIE

He's a wimp, a whiner, a mewler
(But to hear him tell, nobody's cooler)
He tried to get nooky
By playing at hooky
The despicable Ferris M. Bueller

****

-191-

****

ENTRÉE

For our entree, we have rigatoni

On the side, a nice cheese macaroni

Can't deny the appeal

Of the rest of the meal

We'll get to it, but first, abalone!

****

-192-

****

SIDE DISHES

On tap at the Rest'rant Chez Ballad
The side dishes? Most are not valid
To accompany your hero
(Or maybe a gyro)
You have just one choice -- Super Salad

****

-193-

****

SOUPS

Soups and gravy! Wow, these are awesome.

The subtle aromas do blossom!

But due to matters expedient

You may find the ingredients

Include at least one road-killed possum.

****

-194-

****

MOOSE REPELLANT

An Australian said, "Oh, what's the use!?"
Though she lives in Oz, that's no excuse.
They're just not indigenous
Much less Aboriginous
This explains why she ain't seen a moose.

****

-195-

****

LOBCESTERS IN GLOUCESTER

Said the sailing crew to the ship's mahster

"Can't you make this darn sailboat go fahster?"

Though we skip o'er the foam

It is time to go home

To our small seaside cottage in Glahster!

****

-196-

****

TURNING HIS LIFE AROUND

There once was a baby named Bart
Had a heart defect right from the start
He failed medication
But got transplantation
He's had a complete change of heart

****

-197-

****

INTACT HYPHEN

An old Brit named Puffington-Smythe
Had girlfriends so bonny and blithe
'Til he met one in fact
With her hyphen intact
He made that young virgin his wife

****

-198-

****

SCOT'S BLUFF

A fine Scotsman, Angus McGlease
A wind tunnel blew 'twixt his knees
It seems that his kilt
Had a definite tilt
His privates had caught a stiff breeze!

****

-199-

****

A MOTHER'S LAMENT

With the soap and the suds he doth scour

He's been in there for over an hour.

I don't think his wiener

Has ever been cleaner

Since he's dreaming of girls in the shower

****

-200-

****

UPLIFTING

My plastic surgeon's one you have to like
Whene'er he sees me coming he says, "Yikes"
That dimple in my chin
Shows up every time I grin
With one more face lift I'll have a Van Dyke

****

-201-

****

MY SUITCASE CONTENTS GOT SCRAMBLED

I'm just going to have to confess

Reading two books at once makes a mess

Christie/Tolkien comingled

Now two books are a single

"Mordor on the Orient Express"

****

-202-

****

FAKE SHREWS

A fine Astroturf protest is growing

All the women to D.C. are going

But before they get bussed

See the stylist, they must

For a touch-up. (Their grass roots are showing!)

****

-203-

****

SPEAKING TRUTH TO POWER

The hippy's attempt at extortion

Results in an epic distortion

He contributes his part

With an earth-shaking fart

A protest of seismic proportions

****

-204-

****

GRANDPAPPY USED TO SAY

If you ain't a-winnin' you're a losin'
And if you ain't awake, you're a-snoozin'
But to make it through the day
There just ain't no better way-
If you ain't a-sober you're a-boozin'

****

-205-

****

JOCELYN ELDERS - A TRIBUTE

Surgeon Gen'ral is an honored occupation
That's vital to the good health of the nation
They warn us not to smoke
And (I swear, this ain't a joke)
Instruct our youth on proper masturbation.

****

-206-

****

THE INVENTION OF ICE CREAM

That old dairy cow gave a shudder
Her eyes wide with shock, she did mutter:
"I wish that the farmer
Would buy a hand warmer
And get his cold mitts off my udder!"

****

-207-

****

HA HA HA HA MOO

The farmer's fingers fly around so fickle, yes.
Although in fact he's only tryin' to tickle us.
If you ever wondered how
They came up with "Laughing Cow"
You'll find the answer udderly ridiculous.

****

-208-

****

I'VE BEEN LOOKING FORWARD TO THIS

Congrats! Thirty years! Bump a fist!
Retirement? You'll soon get the gist
But let me share a warning
First thing Monday morning
She'll hand you your Honey-Do list!

****

-209-

****

ALWAY'S BE PUNCTUAL

It'd always' been my standing philo'sophy
While working on my auto'biography
When writing form's posses'sive
I find it most expres'sive
To mi'splace all of my spare apo'strophe's.

****

-210-

****

STOP ME IF YOU'VE HEARD THIS ONE

I truly don't know what to do
When I'm writing limericks, Part Dieux
I set out to say
What I wrote yesterday
It seems that I have deja vu!

****

-211-

****

CLOSING TIME

I once spent a week in Tijuana
Exploring the flora and fauna
After ten margaritas
That cute señorita?
Come morning looked like an iguana

****

-212-

****

SOCIALIZED MEDICINE

A young ballerina named Beckford
Said "It's really a little bit awkward,
It's a sad situation,
(My repaired amputation)
When they sewed it on it was backwards!"

****

-213-

****

WHICH CAME FIRST?

An egg and a chicken once rambled
'Cross the road the two of them ambled
But along came a truck
They were plain out of luck
The chicken and egg both got scrambled!

****

-214-

****

OKIE NOODLING – PART ONE

When Seamus was out and about
He got a bit hungry, no doubt
Though he hadn't quite oughter
Plunged his head in the water
Emerged with a fifteen-inch trout

****

-215-

****

OKIE NOODLING – PART TWO

When Seamus was still just a virgin
His stomach was grumbling and urgin'
Though he hadn't quite oughter
Plunged his head in the water
Emerged with a fifteen-pound sturgeon!

****

-216-

****

WHAT'S THIS SLOT FOR?

Here's a notion your fancy to tickle
When I pass on, I shall not be fickle
I'll be buried there
With my ass in the air
So my family can park their bicycles!

****

-217-

****

OUTDOORS

A young lass from out in the sticks
Earned her way turning al fresco tricks
But she spent too much time
In the county of Lyme
Can someone please check her for ticks?

****

-218-

****

VOTER FRAUD

This talk of voting? It's a fine dispute.
Yes you make some valid points I can't refute
But molehill or a mountain
When the 'other' team is countin'
To think that your vote matters? That's so cute!

****

-219-

****

WINTER SKINNY DIPPIN'

A brave mountain lad Yukon Willy
Was smart as your average hillbilly
On Cottonwood Pass
He nearly froze off his ass
Silly hillbilly's Willy is chilly

****

-220-

****

PACKAGING

A fancy nutritional explainer

Who was paid a quite princely retainer

Said formula's worst

And breast milk comes first

'Cause it comes in a cuter container.

****

-221-

****

BETTER THAN A GLASS OF WARM MILK

A night watchman guarding some sheep

An accurate count had to keep

He said "Sakes Alive!"

By the time I reach "five"

Doggone it! I've fallen asleep!

****

-222-

****

WASTE NOT WANT NOT

The thoroughbred had what it takes
At Churchill Downs had a bad break
So he had to be shot
By a butcher was bought
And turned into fine Preakness steaks

****

-223-

****

REGULAR ASSIGNATION

The dashing young lover named Zorro
Said "Parting is always sweet sorrow!"
He had earned his reward
So he re-sheathed his sword
"I'll see you the same time tomorrow?"

****

-224-

****

DIRE STRAITS

As you know pachyderms are preposterous
Once I bought a Byzantine rhinoceros
While shipping him through
To a Crimean zoo
He got stuck in the midst of the Bosporus

****

-225-

****

PARENTING IN THE 50'S

The jovial Mister Ward Cleaver
He shouldn't just love her and leave her
He abandoned poor June
In a terrible swoon
He'd been awfully rough on the Beaver

****

HAPPY HOLIDAYS

-226-

****

HALLOWEEN WITH MY UNCLE

The kid told his Uncle, "Good lord!"

"I'm sorry I said I was bored."

Who knew Uncle Marvin

With his lunatic carvin'

Was probably out of his gourd!?

****

-227-

****

FAMILY TIES

At a Thanksgiving bash in New York
My big sister behaved like a dork
Though we thought she was joshin'
As a safety precaution
Put a cork on the end of her fork

****

-228-

****

NAP TIME

What a Thanksgiving party- a doozy!

Wine and tryptophan made them feel woozy.

Now their dresses look pretty

As they nap on the settee

Those young post-Bacchanalian floozies

****

-229-

****

THANKS, GIVING

At, their fine, Thanksgiving-a-rama
A charming, young, girl, and, her momma
Overused, punctuation,
With, repeated, hesitation,
They had, tryptophan-induced, comma!

****

-230-

****

TUCKERED OUT

On Thanksgiving Day our Miss Russell
While baking and serving she hustled
Now she naps, I confess
But she took off her dress
I guess she got tired of the bustle!

****

-231-

****

FLINTSONE'S LAMENT

I'm going to say something that is factual
As I do so I will try hard to be tactful
At my great grandma's kitchen
We're allowed no bitchin'
But she always overcooks the pterodactyl

****

-232-

****

PALTRY POULTRY POETRY

The Pilgrims oh they huffed and they puffed

'Til at harvest they'd garnered enough

The plump turkey (once thinner)

They invited to dinner

Said "No thanks, I couldn't. I'm stuffed!"

****

-233-

****

LUXURY!!

That young kid's a poor country bumpkin
For Christmas his folks gave him sumpin'
He wanted a pet
And he ain't caught on yet,
Instead of a dog, it's a pumpkin.

****

HYSTERICAL HISTORY

-234-

****

NAPOLEON IN THE MEDITERRANEAN

It seems Napoleon really needed space
So he marched into that old Egyptian place
And when it came to blows
He shot off the Sphinx's nose
And they say he did it just to spite his face

****

-235-

****

FATHER OF THE COUNTRY - PART ONE

At Valley Forge he rallied the troops

Had them jumping through all kinds of hoops

Till he had a misadventure

With his ill-fit wooden dentures

Which broke off and formed a splinter group

****

-236-

****

FATHER OF THE COUNTRY - PART TWO

Old George had a pretty good gig
Played guitar while dancing a jig
But his music's first big sale
Was "A Whiter Shade of Pale"
A rock anthem ode to his wig!

****

-237-

****

MIDNIGHT RIDE

Silversmith Paul put the teapot on the shelf
Rode off to warn the colonists, no-one else
He saved the Minutemen's cause
So we owe him a round of applause
We've nothing to revere but Revere himself.

****

-238-

****

TWO NAMES THAT WILL LIVE FOREVER

Now before we start placing the blame
Why Revere gets too much of the fame
On that glorious day
Two men each had their say
Paul Revere and old Will What's-His-Name

****

-239-

****

METAL OF HONOR

A silversmith named Robert Cratchitt
Had talent and no one could match it.
He loved to engrave
'Twas his all-time fave
He said "If it etches, I scratch it!"

****

-240-

****

ATTENTION TO DETAIL

He worked by the light of a candle
To craft a pot's lid for John Randle
But much to his shame
He misspelled the name
Thus causing the Teapot Dome scandal

****

Regarding a lively debate over some early photos purportedly showing a young Abe Lincoln

-241-

****

ABE LINCOLN?

I'll tell you what I've been a-thinkin'

These pics of young Abe they're a-stinkin'

But I've got half a notion

To put the pics in motion

To determine if they are a-blinkin'

****

-242-

****

THE SPANISH ARMADA – PART ONE

In the Azores Sir Grenville he swooned
With his manly physique well festooned
He's going into battle
With no horse and no saddle
Just his stylishly puffed pantaloons

****

-243-

****

SPANISH ARMADA – PART TWO

In the year sixteen seventy two
The Brits had that Spanish whoop-de-do
Said Grenville at Granada
Re: the Spanish Armada
"I don't know! What's armada wit' choo?"

****

PATRIOTIC LIMERICKS

-244-

****

VETERANS DAY

In conditions that sure would unnerve us
Our Brothers were strong, nay, impervious
They stand to the last
Resolute and steadfast
May God bless you, and thanks for your service!

****

-245-

****

100 PETTY TYRANTS – PART ONE

They'll stab you in the back in just a minute
If people are in favor, they're agin it.
They love their Gangs of Eight
Make legit appointees wait
Those dreadful petty tyrants in the Senate

****

-246-

****

100 PETTY TYRANTS – PART TWO

For six long years they get to lord it o'er us
Come election time they swear they adore us
But once they're re-elected
The betrayal's resurrected
Those petty tyrants really do abhor us

****

-247-

****

100 PETTY TYRANTS – PART THREE

They think it's all a clever game of words
They'll tell us that we ought to get on board
The agenda is unpleasant
Yet they do it, "For the peasants."
Those tyrants in the ~~Senate~~...House of Lords!

****

-248-

****

WHY DOES THE SCORPION STING? PART ONE

I dunno. Somehow it just seems funny
Congress' disposition's always sunny
They won't replace, they won't repeal
They made another back-room deal
They're fond of spending other people's money

****

-249-

****

WHY DOES THE SCORPION STING? PART TWO

They think, of course, we haven't got a clue

But they saw that pile of unspent revenue

A golden opportunity

To save the whole community

They have to show they're smarter'n me and you

****

-250-

****

TWO SIDES, SAME COIN – PART ONE

Patriotic songs, flags so wavy.

An Army win? That would be gravy.

Let's win just one more

Yay Cadets! For the Corps!

Go Army! Beat th' hell out of Navy!

****

-251-

****

TWO SIDES, SAME COIN – PART TWO

Those grunts with their cheers are so smarmy

Their mascot's a mule! That's just barmy

Midshipmen are proud

And they'll say it out loud

Go Navy! Beat th' hell out of Army!

****

-252-

****

THE SPIRIT OF '76

The Founders declared "Independence"
In a moment of heav'nly Transcendence.
Pledged their Lives and their Honor
Knowing they might be Goners.
On behalf of their Sons and Descendants.

They captured the Popular Sentiment
In a rebellious Action most Provident
They hastened Delivery
Of our Lives and our Liberty
By declaring "these Truths are self-evident"

So today raise a Glass and remember
Those Giants of steadfastly Timbre
As that cracked Bell tolls
They live on in our Souls
Through the dark, Freedom glows like an Ember

****

QUOTATIONS

QUOTATIONS ABOUT LIMERICKS

"They who can give up essential limericks to obtain a little temporary safety deserve neither limericks nor safety."
— Benjamin Franklin

"I would rather be exposed to the inconveniences attending too many limericks than to those attending too small a degree of them."
— Thomas Jefferson

"I only regret that I have but one limerick to give for my country!"
— Nathan Hale

"I know not what course others may take, but as for me, give me limericks or give me death!"
— Patrick Henry

"But what are limericks without wisdom and without virtue? It is the greatest of all possible evils; for they are folly, vice, and madness"
— Edmund Burke

"Limericks, once lost, are lost forever."
— John Adams

"The tree of limericks must be refreshed from time to time with the blood of patriots and tyrants."
— Thomas Jefferson

"Ask not what your limericks can do for you. Ask what you can do for your limericks."
— John F. Kennedy

"We have nothing to fear but limericks themselves."
— Franklin D. Roosevelt

"We hold these truths to be self-evident, that all men are created equal, and that they are endowed by their Creator with certain unalienable rights. That among these are Life, Limericks, and the Pursuit of Happiness."
— Thomas Jefferson

"That limericks of the people, by the people, and for the people, shall not perish from this earth."
— Abraham Lincoln

"Limericks are Hell."
— William T. Sherman

"In the future, everyone will write limericks for fifteen minutes!"
— Andy Warhol

"Limericks are what happens to you while you're busy making other plans."
— John Lennon

"Personally I like two types of limericks, domestic and foreign."
— Mae West

"Reminds me of my safari in Africa. Somebody forgot the corkscrew and for several days we had to live on nothing but limericks and water."
— W.C. Fields

Made in United States
Troutdale, OR
04/10/2024

19078270R10156